2 CDs INCLUDED

154 TRACKS!

GROOVES YOU CAN USE

154 ESSENTIAL DRUMBEATS IN POPULAR STYLES

BY SCOTT SCHROEDL

ISBN-13: 978-1-4234-2106-1
ISBN-10: 1-4234-2106-X

HAL•LEONARD®
CORPORATION

7777 W. BLUEMOUND RD. P.O. BOX 13819 MILWAUKEE, WI 53213

In Australia Contact:
Hal Leonard Australia Pty. Ltd.
4 Lentara Court
Cheltenham, Victoria, 3192 Australia
Email: ausadmin@halleonard.com

Visit Hal Leonard Online at
www.halleonard.com

ABOUT THIS BOOK

This book provides notation for each drumbeat in a variety of styles. The beats are organized into four large categories (classic rock, modern rock, hip-hop & rap, and additional styles), with each category broken down into a multitude of sub-styles. For the composing musician or novice drummer, this book may serve as a hands-on dictionary of genuine grooves in these styles.

DRUMSET LEGEND

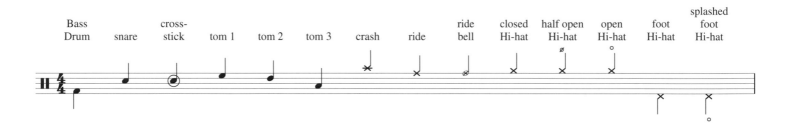

ABOUT THE CDs

The accompanying two audio CDs contain tracks for every groove in the book. Each beat is preceded by a measure of "clicks" to indicate tempo and meter. The CD track icons correspond to the CD and track number for each beat.

CD 1 • Track 1

Contents

RECORDING CREDITS

Recorded, mixed, and mastered by Jake Johnson and John Machnik.
All drum parts performed by Scott Schroedl.

ACKNOWLEDGMENTS

Special thanks go out to the following people for helping me to make music my life: My wife, Melyssa, for her inspiration, friendship, love, and constant support in my life and musical endeavors; my parents, Ed and Jean Schroedl, for allowing me to practice my drums whenever I wanted to while growing up in their house; my first drum teacher, Evan Fisher, for inspiring me to always play my best; all of the musicians I've had the pleasure to play with over the years; my students, past and present, for allowing me to shape their musical minds; Roy Burns and Chris Brady at Aquarian Drumheads; Darrell Johnston and Karen at Axis Pedals; Ed Clift, Andrew Shreve, and Erik Paiste at Paiste Cymbals; Jay and Carol Jones at Noble & Cooley Drums; Vic Firth, Bobbie Bartlett, Neil Larrivee, Rudy Gowern at Vic Firth Drumsticks; Patrick Cunningham, Michael Davidson, and Tom Henry at Drum Tech; and everyone at Hal Leonard Corporation.

Classic Rock

Rock 'n' Roll

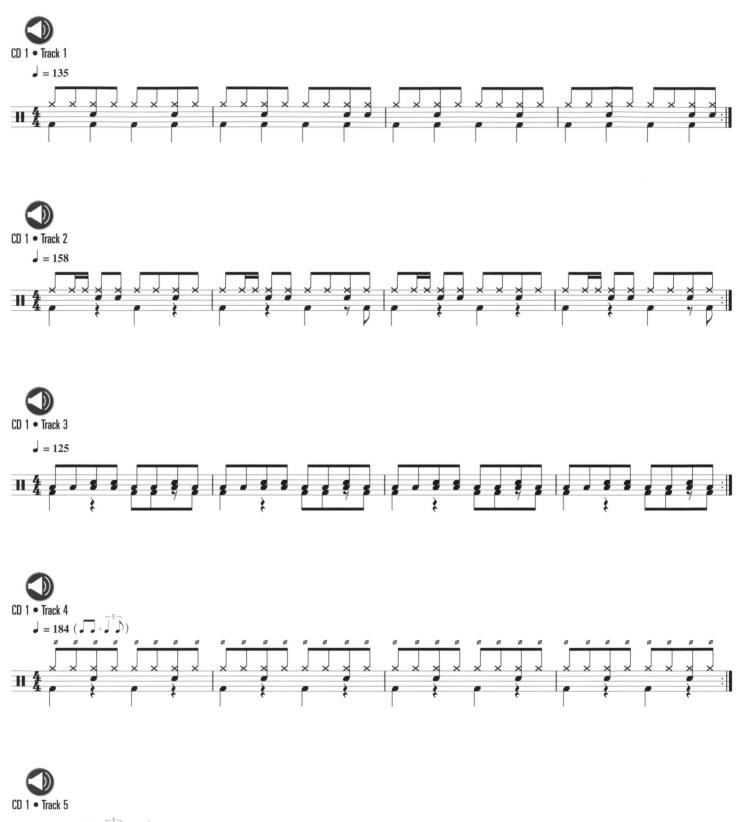

CD 1 • Track 1

♩ = 135

CD 1 • Track 2

♩ = 158

CD 1 • Track 3

♩ = 125

CD 1 • Track 4

♩ = 184 (♫ = ♩♪)

CD 1 • Track 5

♩ = 170 (♫ = ♩♪) (✗ = snare rim)

R R L L L R R L L R L R L L   R R L L R R L L   R R L L R L R L L

Surf

CD 1 • Track 6

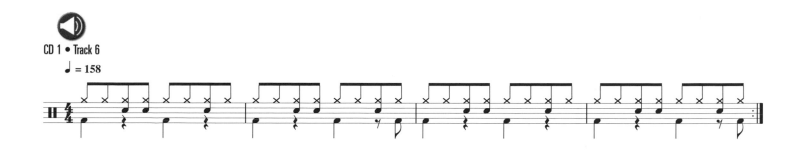

CD 1 • Track 7

CD 1 • Track 8

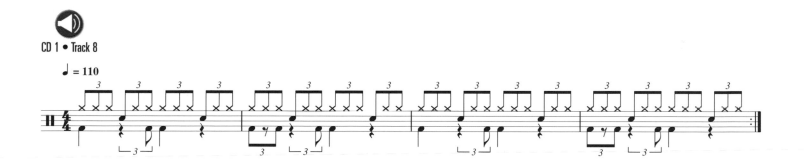

CD 1 • Track 9

'50s Rock

'60s Rock

Classic Rock

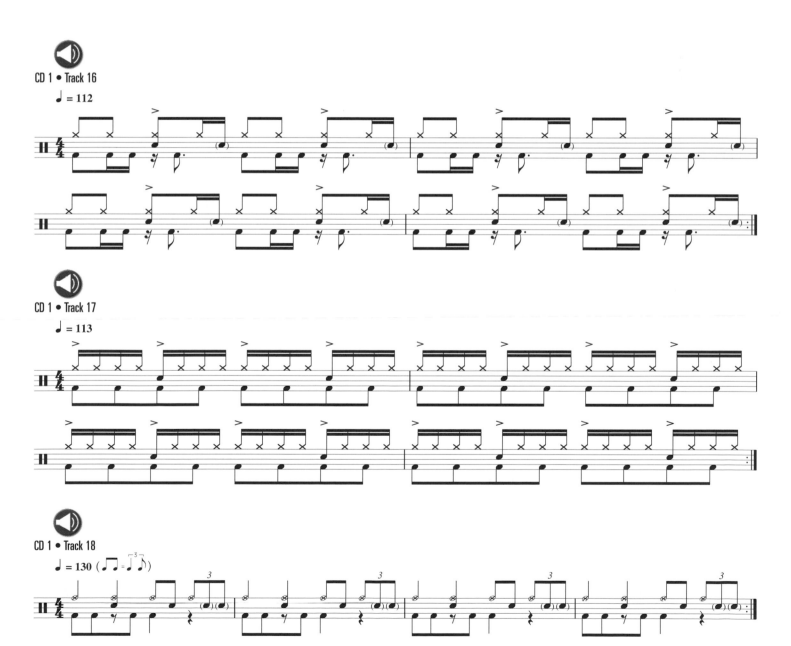

'70s Rock

Hard Rock

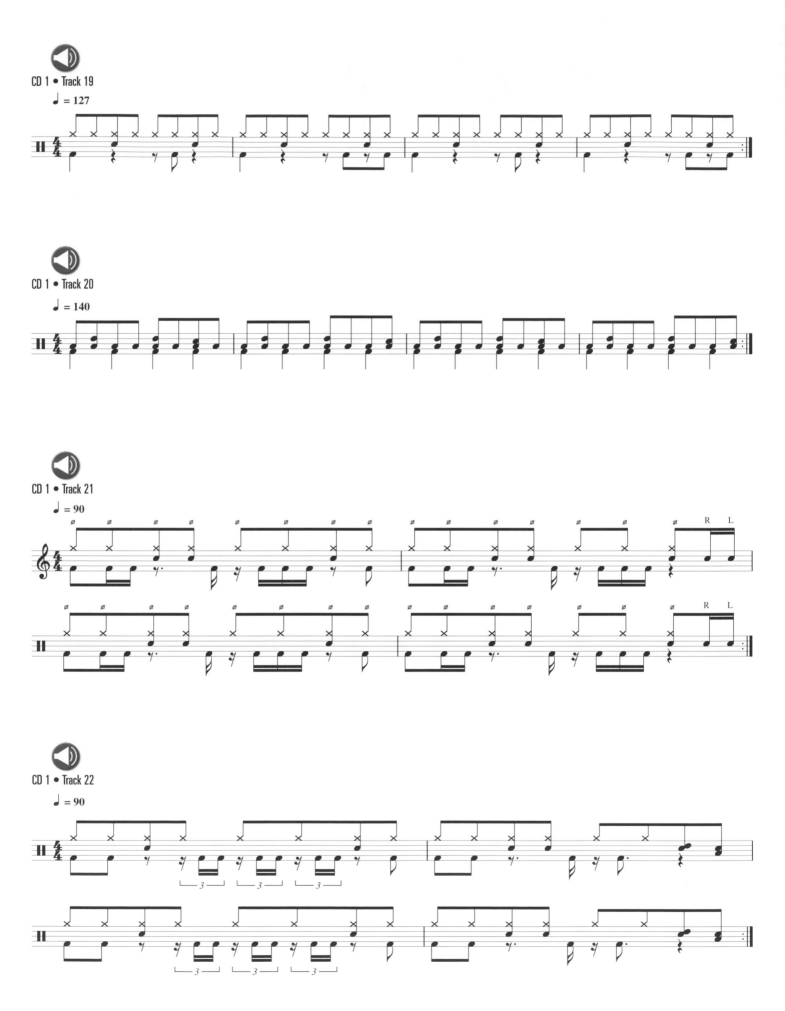

CD 1 • Track 19

♩ = 127

CD 1 • Track 20

♩ = 140

CD 1 • Track 21

♩ = 90

CD 1 • Track 22

♩ = 90

Classic Rock

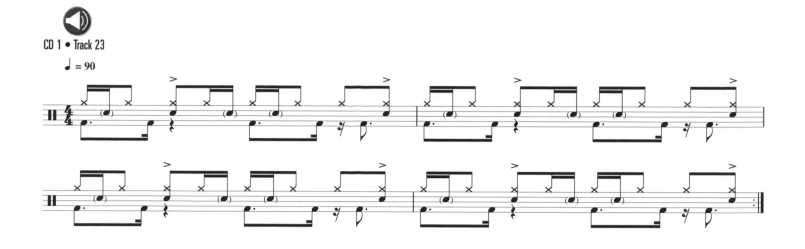

CD 1 • Track 23

$\quad$ = 90

Pop Rock

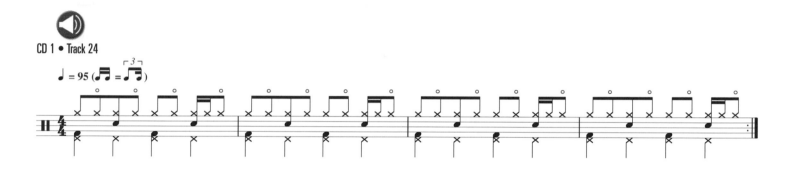

CD 1 • Track 24

$\quad$ = 95

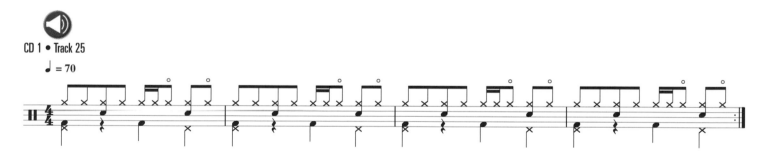

CD 1 • Track 25

$\quad$ = 70

CD 1 • Track 26

$\quad$ = 150

CD 1 • Track 27

$\quad$ = 225

Country Rock

CD 1 • Track 28

♩ = 170

CD 1 • Track 29

♩ = 125

Southern Rock

CD 1 • Track 30

♩ = 180

CD 1 • Track 31

♩ = 190

Power Pop

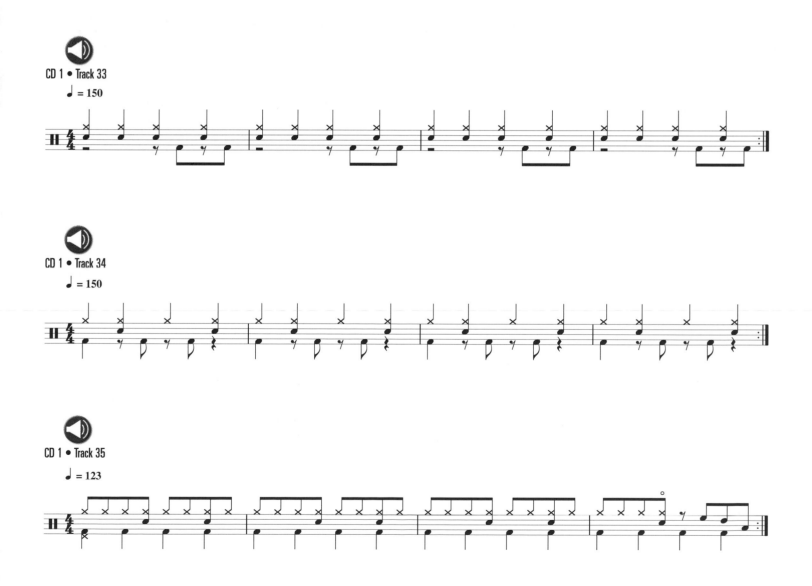

Folk Rock

CD 1 • Track 36

♩ = 100

CD 1 • Track 37

♩ = 120 (✗ = snare rim)

Latin Rock

CD 1 • Track 38

♩ = 110 (snares off)

CD 1 • Track 39

♩ = 120

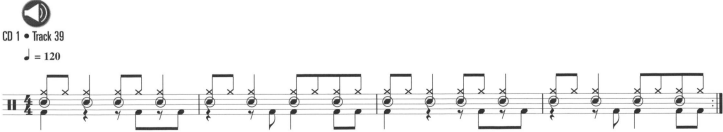

CD 1 • Track 40

♩ = 120 (snares off)

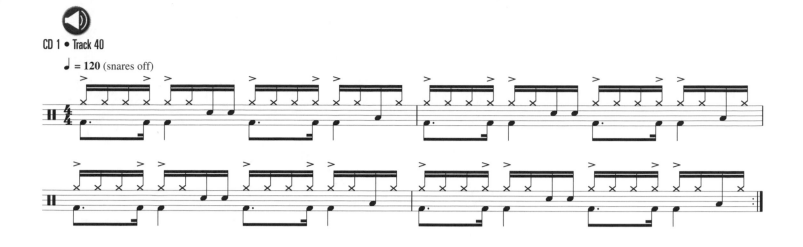

Punk

CD 1 • Track 41

♩ = 114

CD 1 • Track 42

♩ = 168

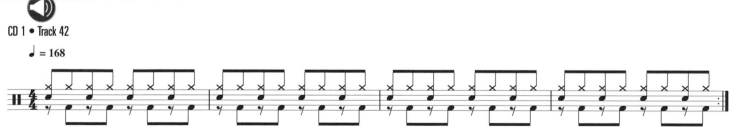

Heavy Metal

American Rock

CD 1 • Track 46

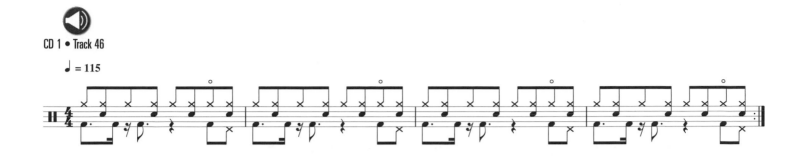

Speed Metal

CD 1 • Track 47

CD 1 • Track 48

CD 1 • Track 49

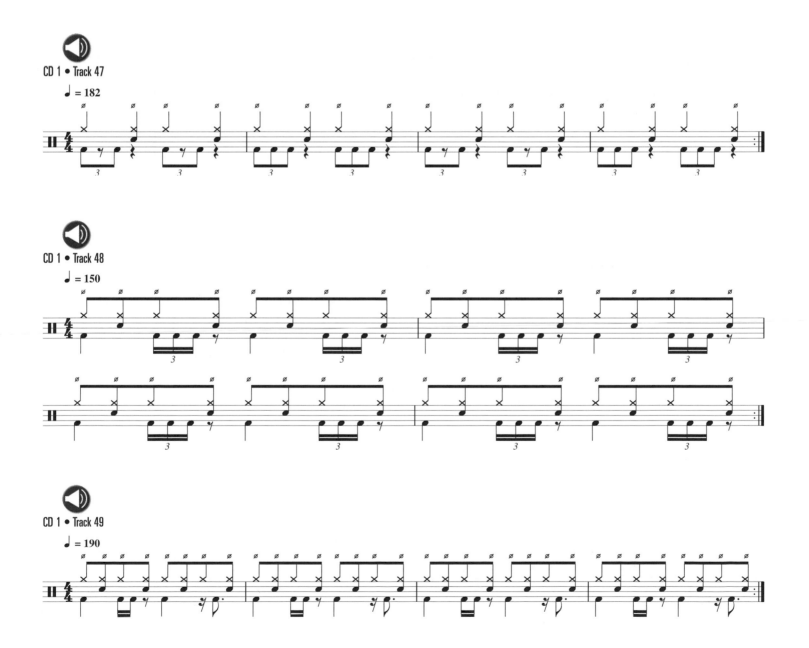

Modern Rock

Mainstream Pop

CD 1 • Track 50

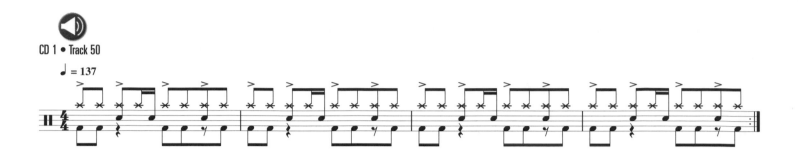

CD 1 • Track 51

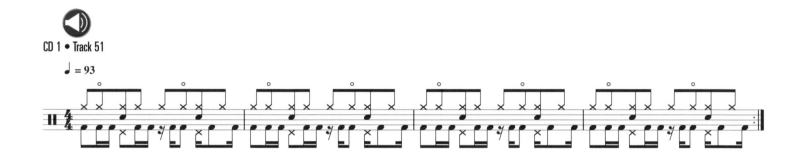

CD 1 • Track 52

CD 1 • Track 53

CD 1 • Track 54

CD 1 • Track 55

CD 1 • Track 56

Modern Metal

CD 1 • Track 57

♩ = 89

CD 1 • Track 58

♩ = 89

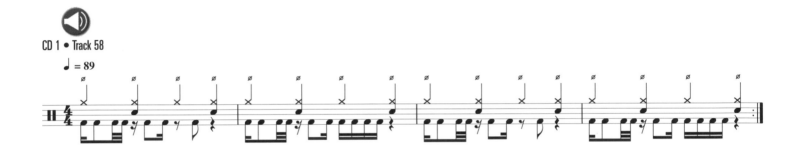

CD 1 • Track 59

♩ = 117

CD 1 • Track 60

♩ = 142

Grunge Rock

CD 1 • Track 61

♩ = 101

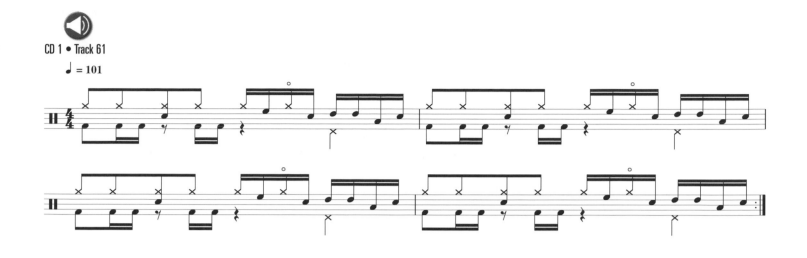

CD 1 • Track 62

♩ = 90

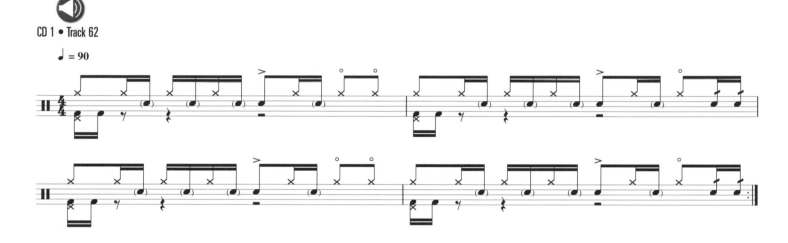

CD 1 • Track 63

♩ = 117

CD 1 • Track 64

♩ = 93

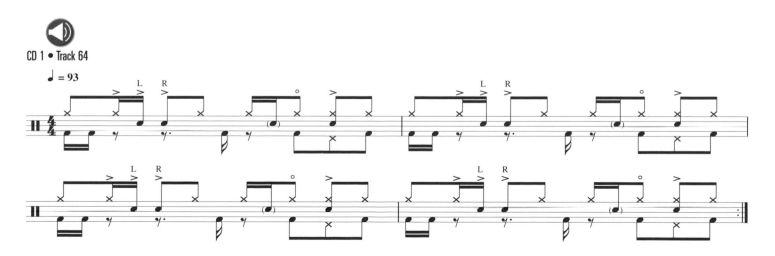

CD 1 • Track 65

♩ = 107

CD 1 • Track 66

♩ = 98

Alternate Rock

CD 1 • Track 67

♩ = 103

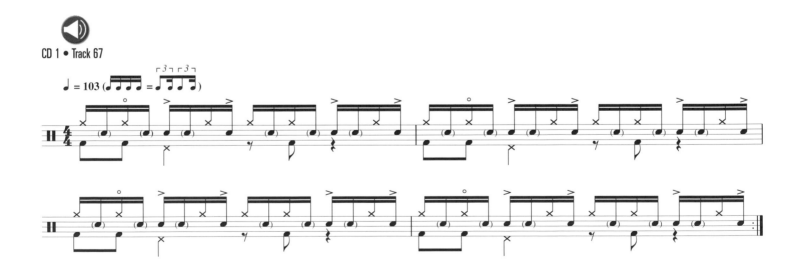

CD 1 • Track 71

$\quad$ = 163

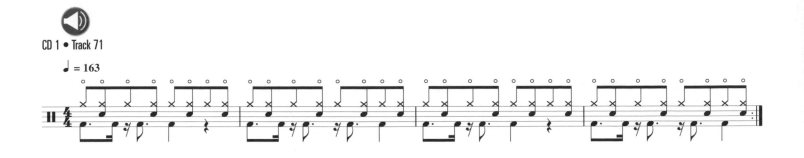

CD 1 • Track 72

$\quad$ = 219

CD 1 • Track 73

$\quad$ = 123

CD 1 • Track 74

$\quad$ = 85

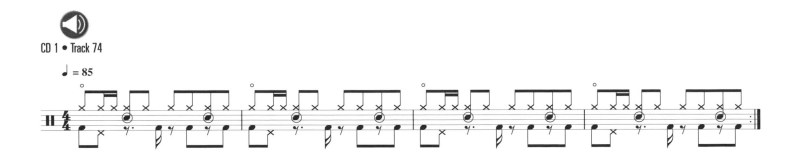

CD 1 • Track 75

♪ = 208

CD 1 • Track 76

♩ = 82

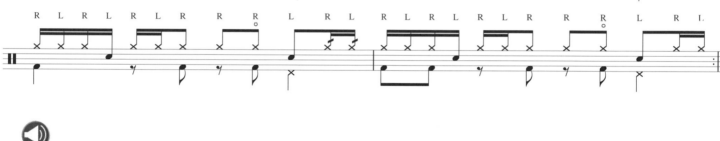

CD 1 • Track 77

♩ = 110

CD 1 • Track 78

♩ = 108

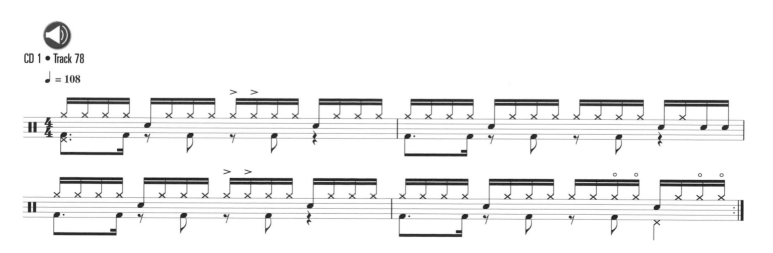

Modern Rock

Blues Rock

CD 1 • Track 79

CD 1 • Track 80

CD 1 • Track 81

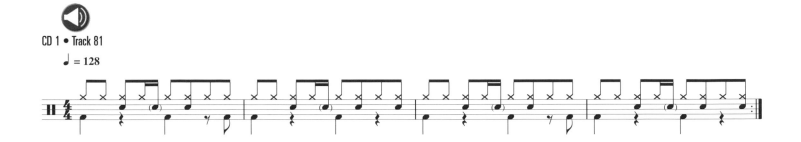

Modern Rock

Progressive Rock

CD 1 • Track 82

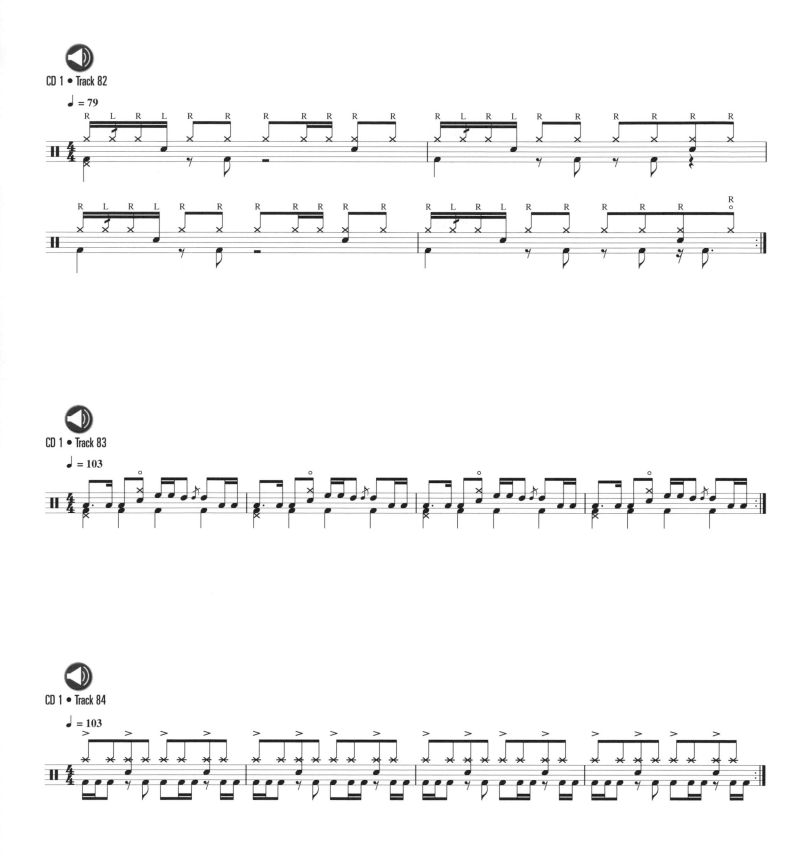

CD 1 • Track 83

CD 1 • Track 84

Hard Rock

CD 1 • Track 85

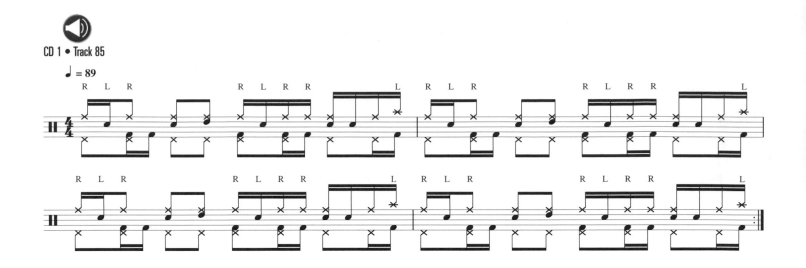

CD 1 • Track 86

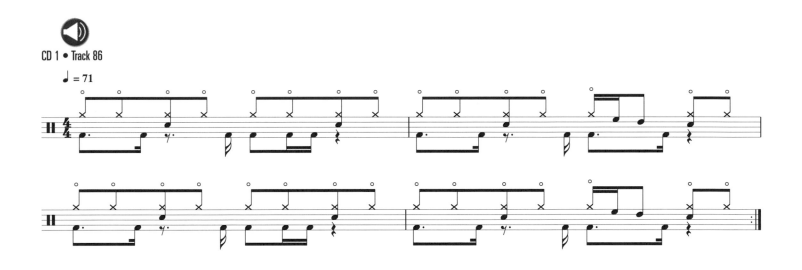

CD 1 • Track 87

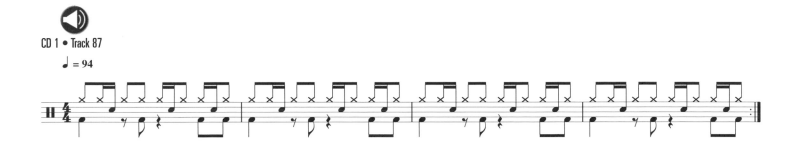

Modern Rock

Funk Rock

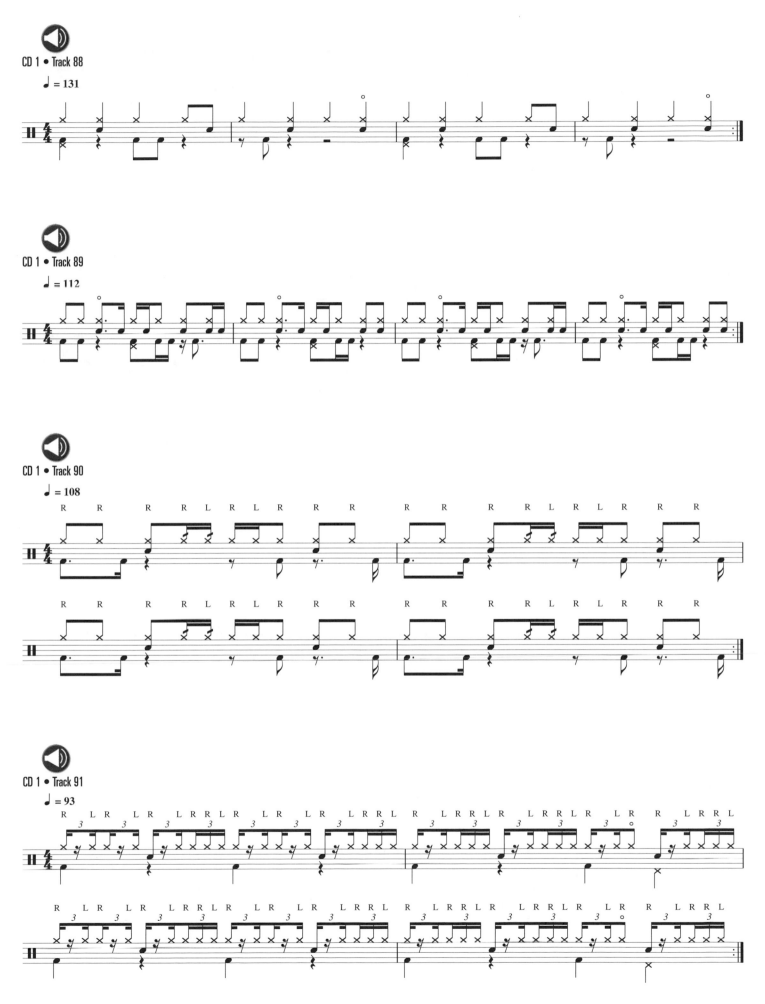

CD 1 • Track 92

♩ = 123

CD 1 • Track 93

♩ = 92 (♪♪ = ³♪♪)

Ska

CD 1 • Track 94

♩ = 150

CD 1 • Track 95

♩ = 188

R L R L LL R L R L   R L R L R L R L R LL   R L R L R L R L R LL   R L R L LL R L R LL

Hip-Hop & Rap

East Coast

CD 2 • Track 6

West Coast

CD 2 • Track 7

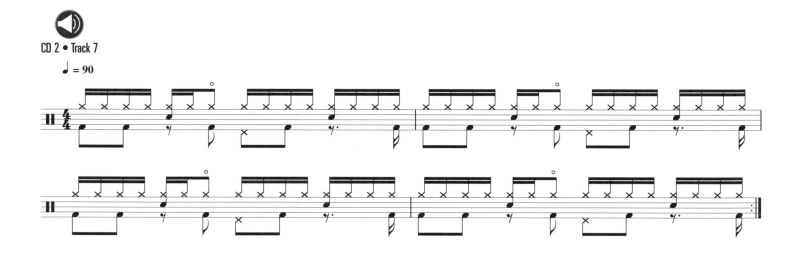

CD 2 • Track 8

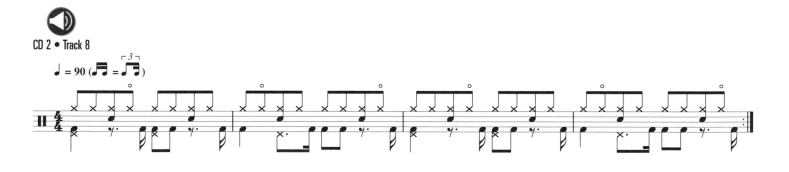

CD 2 • Track 9

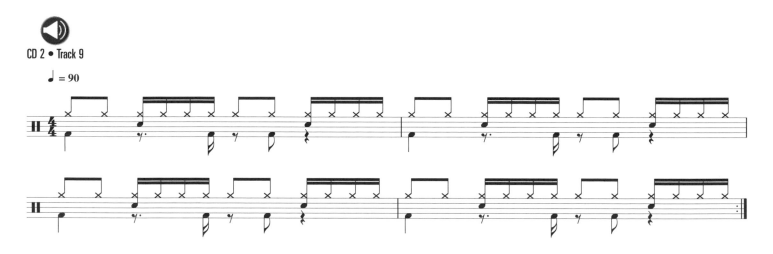

Down South

CD 2 • Track 10

♩ = 75

CD 2 • Track 11

♩ = 86 (♫ = ⌐3⌐)

CD 2 • Track 12

♩ = 103 (♫ = ⌐3⌐)

Old School

CD 2 • Track 13

♩ = 95 (♫ = ⌐3⌐)

CD 2 • Track 14

♩ = 108 (♫ = ⌐3⌐)

Pop R&B

CD 2 • Track 15

CD 2 • Track 16

CD 2 • Track 17

CD 2 • Track 18

Additional Styles

Blues

CD 2 • Track 19

♩ = 132

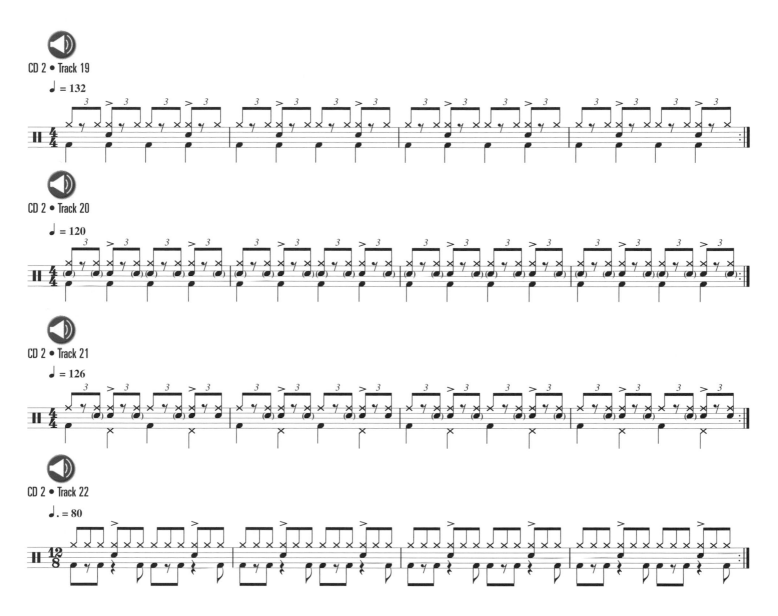

CD 2 • Track 20

♩ = 120

CD 2 • Track 21

♩ = 126

CD 2 • Track 22

♩. = 80

Bossa Nova

CD 2 • Track 23

♩ = 144

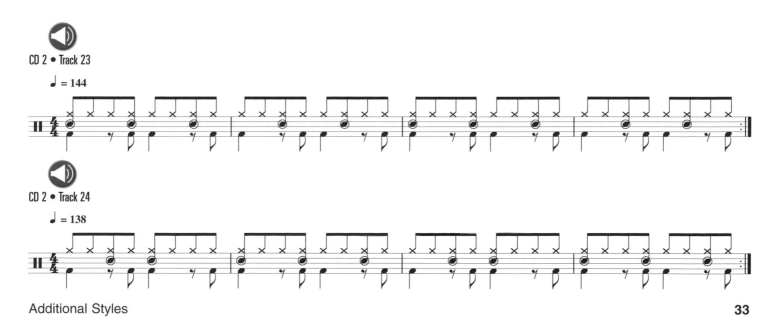

CD 2 • Track 24

♩ = 138

Cha-Cha

CD 2 • Track 25

♩ = 126

Country

CD 2 • Track 26

♩ = 216

Disco

CD 2 • Track 27

♩ = 132

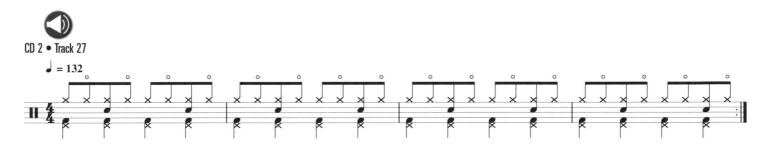

CD 2 • Track 28

♩ = 120

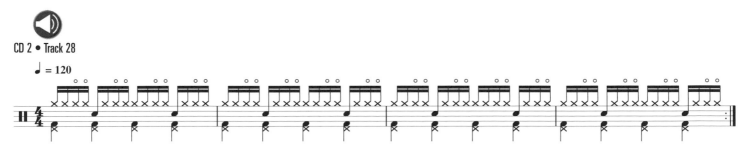

CD 2 • Track 29

♩ = 138

Funk

Gospel

Mambo

The right hand should be played on a cowbell, but you could substitute the ride cymbal bell if you don't have one.

CD 2 • Track 35

♩ = 208

CD 2 • Track 36

♩ = 184

Motown

CD 2 • Track 37

♩ = 120

CD 2 • Track 38

♩ = 120

CD 2 • Track 39

♩ = 120

New Orleans

♩ = 168

♩ = 200

♩ = 168

Punk

♩ = 176

♩ = 160

R&B/Soul

CD 2 • Track 45

Reggae

CD 2 • Track 47

CD 2 • Track 48

CD 2 • Track 49

Additional Styles

Samba

CD 2 • Track 50

♩ = 92

CD 2 • Track 51

♩ = 88

CD 2 • Track 52

♩ = 132

Soul

CD 2 • Track 53

♩ = 104

CD 2 • Track 54

♩ = 92

CD 2 • Track 55

♩ = 112

Swing/Jazz

CD 2 • Track 56

♩ = 216

CD 2 • Track 57

♩ = 200

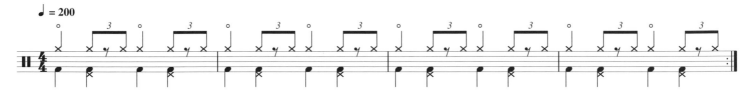

CD 2 • Track 58

♩ = 116

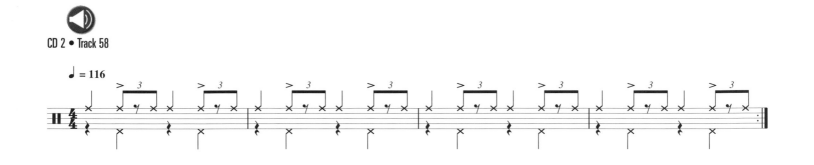

CD 2 • Track 59

♩ = 120

Additional Styles